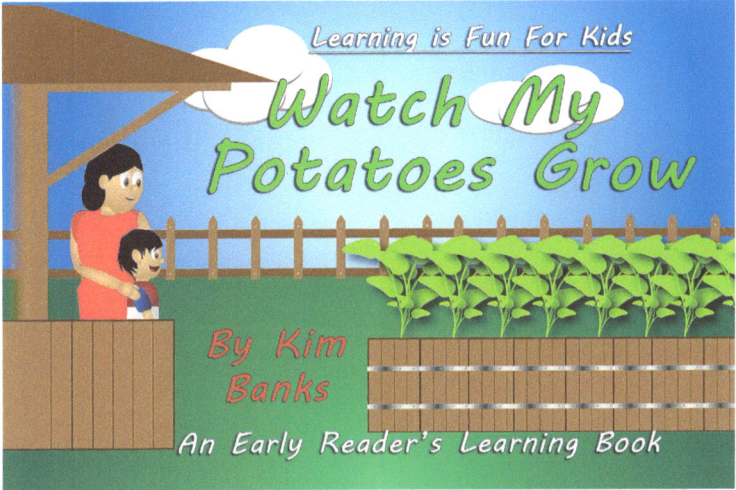

Learning is Fun For Kids

Watch My Potatoes Grow

By Kim Banks

An Early Reader's Learning Book

Dreamstone Publishing © 2015

www.dreamstonepublishing.com

ISBN: 1925165361

ISBN-13: 978-1-925165-36-4

Other Books in the

"Learning is Fun for Kids ....."
Series – Coming Soon

"Who Lives in My Garden ?"

"The Farm Field Trip"

"Cheering Up Eggplant"

The Learning is Fun for Kids
Book Series

This series is designed for early readers – Ages 4 to 8. The stories are fun, but educational, and are designed to encourage discussion and exploration.

KIM BANKS

Watch My Potatoes Grow

It was a warm day, when the sun had just reached its highest point.

I sat doing homework and began to think of other things

"Mom" I said to my mother, who was cooking dinner behind me, "How do potatoes grow?"

"How about we grow some and find out?" She replied

I nodded my head and she raced to the computer to order all of the needed supplies.

We bought bright blue potatoes because of their pretty color.

It took nearly two weeks for them to arrive, but it was worth the wait.

"Ready to grow some potatoes?"

My mother said one Saturday morning.

First we cut the potatoes into 1 inch chunks.

With a one pound bag of seed potatoes it was a lot of chopping!

My mom said that we'd plant them in barrels, to keep them away from our dog, and the neighborhood cats.

We found tons of large barrels in my uncle's store shed!

After cutting the potatoes into chunks, we let them rest in a small corner in the garage, to grow sprouts, while we worked on getting our barrels ready!

"Almost time to plant them!"

My mother said a week later.

Our blue potatoes were starting to sprout!

My uncle came to visit and helped us plant all of the sprouted seed potatoes.

It was

Awesome !

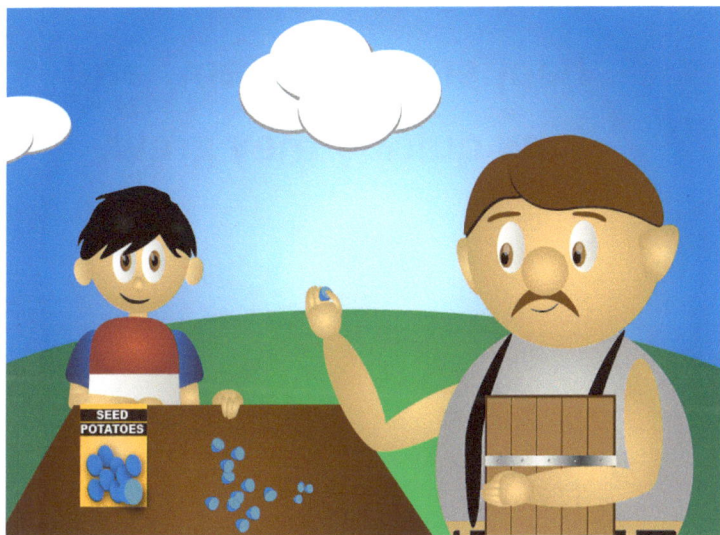

I checked my potatoes daily, to see what happened to them, and how quickly they grew.

Leaves quickly grew from them and it seemed like soon we'd have fresh potatoes to cook with.

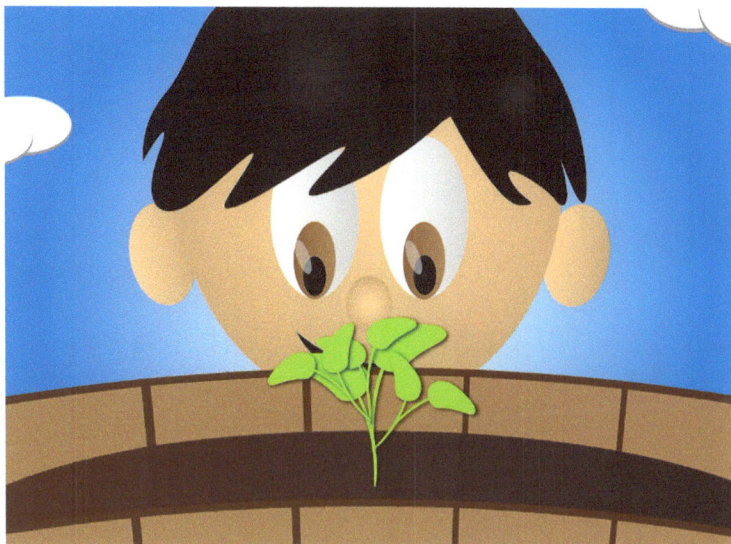

Two months later, my mother and I were harvesting our potatoes from the barrels in the back yard!

"Mom! Look at how blue they are!"

I screamed at the top of my lungs!

"I think that tonight is the night that we taste our harvest and make some burgers with blue potato chips!" said Mom.

"Can we grow lettuce
next?"

I asked my mother.

"Yes" she agreed with a
warm smile, as we sat
and enjoyed eating the
potatoes that we had
worked so hard to grow.

Thank You For Buying This Book !

I hope that you have enjoyed it.

Please leave us a review on Amazon and let us know what you thought !

Leaving reviews on Amazon helps other readers discover good books.

ABOUT THE AUTHOR

Kim Banks is a mother who gave up her corporate job to work from home.

She enjoys writing of all kinds, but is most passionate about creating books that encourage kids to read, and to learn, and to have fun doing it!

Other Books from Dreamstone Publishing

Dreamstone publishes books in a wide variety of categories – here are some of our other bestselling books:-

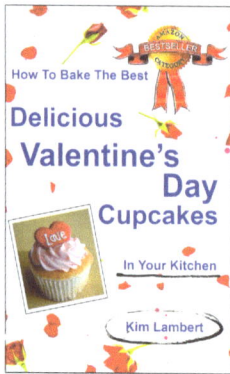

How to Bake the Best Delicious Valentine's Day Cupcakes - In Your Kitchen

By Kim Lambert

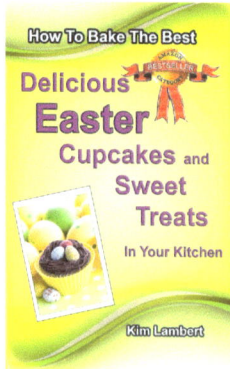

How to Bake the Best Delicious Easter Cupcakes and Sweet Treats - In Your Kitchen

By Kim Lambert

(Also available in Spanish)

The "How to Bake the Best……" Series.

All Books available from all Amazon sites and other good book stores, and available for Kindle too!

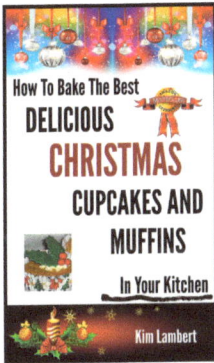

How to Bake the Best

Delicious Christmas

Cupcakes and Muffins - In

Your Kitchen

By Kim Lambert

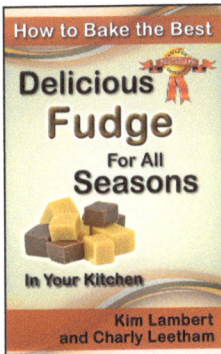

How to Bake the Best

Delicious Fudge For All

Seasons - In Your Kitchen

By Kim Lambert
and Charly Leetham

www.ingramcontent.com/pod-product-compliance
Lightning Source LLC
LaVergne TN
LVHW010024070426
835508LV00001B/40